And together they are strong

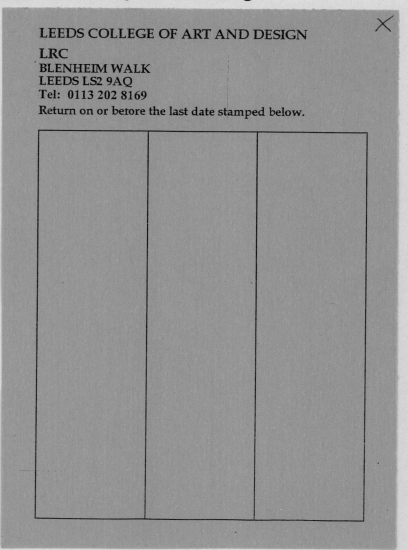

9773

And together they are strong

Rein Wolfs

In their curriculum vitae for the School of Fine Art at the University of Dundee, Tracy Mackenna and Edwin Janssen state that since 1997 they have been working together and no longer produce individual work. And indeed since that time we have encountered their names exclusively as an artistic couple. Within the world of contemporary art that is no exceptional situation. Since the emergence of Gilbert & George and Peter Fischli & David Weiss there has been little doubt that the artistic duo can be a very successful phenomenon.

In our consumer society a name comprising two surnames is quickly assumed to refer to a firm of solicitors, a department store or a clothing brand. Mackenna and Janssen – you can almost see the logo. An equal partnership suggests a certain diversification, but also gives the reassuring message of "strength in numbers". The fact that two partners get along so well inspires trust and gives the impression of a united front against possible hostility from without. Two are better than one. And together they are strong. And they do everything in tandem – very contemporary – according to the rules of a meaningful and well-considered division of labour in order to achieve optimum responsibility.

Tracy Mackenna and Edwin Janssen are not the proprietors of a department store, neither are they partners in a law firm, but they are certainly contemporary. Their collaboration is a discursive association, a method that within their profession – contemporary art – is extremely valuable, for various reasons.

Since the advent of Conceptual Art, art has shifted from doing to thinking, from craft to idea. In the new art, driven by ideas, the thought process has become ever more an integral part of the artistic process. And thinking is an activity that is more likely to lead to something new when done in a pair rather than alone. Mackenna and Janssen are each other's *Gegenüber* as the Germans so appositely put it. They are each other's sounding board and sparring partner. They are able to test, contradict and refine each other's ideas and to develop them further.

Tracy Mackenna and Edwin Janssen are clear representatives of an art form that has been dubbed *relational aesthetics* by the French curator and theoretician Nicolas Bourriaud. He employs this term to denote a form of art that privileges the development of relationships, namely the relationship between the artist and the viewer by means of the work of art. This relationship is thematised and developed – in economic terms – as a *unique selling point*. In order to optimise the relationship with the viewer, it is important that Mackenna and Janssen can continuously hone their communication and collaboration, both with and without public interference. Their private discourse is an important basis for their relational activities, for their direct communication with the public.

Tracy and Edwin complement one another. Over the years they have adopted a shared direction, but they clearly remain two people with two different names. For some of their works they use the pseudonym *Ed and Ellis*, which functions even more like a logo thanks to its brevity and alliteration. When working in Tokyo, a culture of speed, this *'faster'* double nomenclature enabled them to access the couleur locale with greater ease – with a sort of cartoon-like haste.

As 'relationists' Mackenna and Janssen almost always make an appearance on site, where their work *takes place* in the literal sense. In contrast to many art forms, in which the artist *appears* or *performs*, within the visual arts the artist is rarely present in the gallery space during an exhibition. Mackenna and Janssen, however, appear *live* in their own installations. In a kind of real-time situation they attempt to make their engagement manifest. Their presence does not cease after the private view, but continues throughout the two or three months of any given exhibition. Thus they embody – substantially – the ultimate authenticity of the artist, and mediate between the work of art and the public themselves rather than leaving this to the institution's education department, as is usually the case.

Within the world of the visual arts, direct communication

with the public is normally the role of educators or indeed the work of art itself. The artist is the maker of the artefact – whether that is an object, an installation or anything else – and that artefact must be capable of holding its own with a third party, without the requirement for the maker to be present. At the moment when, as it were, a contract is struck between the work and the consumer, the producer has long left the scene. Of course this is usually the case in the real world – as opposed to the cultural world – but that concerns mass-produced items that are judged on their function. The product's uniqueness and the maker's individuality are here of little significance. By contrast with art these qualities are of the greatest importance. And exactly in the realm of art, at the critical moment when the communicative contract is signed, the authentic figure of the maker is absent. Strange really...

The *relationists* such as Mackenna and Janssen are often present at, or indeed within their own product, allowing them to influence the reception of their work in a more immediate manner. That is not always as simple as it may seem because public expectation is by no means always willing to have its reception influenced by the maker. Not every museum visitor wishes to be interactive and to have his or her contemplative state interfered with. Art is all too often associated with a merely visual activity, a somewhat old-fashioned view, I would argue.

Take to the streets

In the first years of their collaboration much of Tracy and Edwin's work took place in the street. In search of a high level of reality and social commitment, in the late 1990s they opted to pursue a relationship with the social environment. In one sense they seek a *linguistic* connection with the socio-political environment. In several text-based works they identified with John Lennon and Yoko Ono by appropriating their slogan '*WAR IS OVER! If you want it*'. John and Yoko stand for a beautiful sort of vagueness:

their oracle-like statements contain a naive idealism conveyed in a propagandistic manner. Consequently when Mackenna and Janssen wrote '*WMD ARE THERE! If you want it*', they were referring to Tony Blair's justification for the war against Iraq because of the purported presence of Weapons of Mass Destruction. And with '*LIFE IS OVER! If you want it*' they tackled the problem of euthanasia, which is still illegal in Great Britain.

If the text works have a certain conceptual character, several of their artistic activities take place literally in the social environment. With reference to a form of 1960s and 1970s political activism, Tracy and Edwin, or rather Ed and Ellis as they often called themselves in this period, literally took to the streets. They leafleted and fly posted, canvassed the public to vote for a non-existent politician, used seductive offers to tempt passers-by into the museum, and engaged with the public as researchers or, more accurately, field workers.

Years before the populist right-winger Pim Fortuyn would so dramatically shake up Dutch society, Mackenna and Janssen produced an art work in which they denounced the marketing strategies and mechanisms of populist politics. Fortuyn was assassinated in May 2002, after he had won a massive victory in the elections for the Rotterdam City Council and stood on the brink of national power. His call for a new *quality of life* in Rotterdam and the Netherlands brought about a political upheaval. Fortuyn's legacy is now being implemented in large sections of Dutch society: a zero tolerance security policy, an increasing dismantlement of the notion of a multicultural society and destruction of cultural aspirations.

With '*Ed and Ellis in Schiedam*' in 1998 Mackenna and Janssen introduced a sort of Fortuyn avant la lettre, a fictitious candidate in the elections for the City Council of Schiedam, the old city neighbouring Rotterdam. Having no idea that within just a few years populist right-wing politics would become so socially acceptable in the Netherlands, and particularly in Rotterdam, with Koos van der Sluis they created a caricature of this type of urbane politician. Thus they attempted to make a connection between the real social situation of the local council elections and the cultural situation of an exhibition at the Stedelijk Museum Schiedam. Because they came into conflict with other political parties whilst fly-posting their *Koos van der Sluis* election posters, they made sure that the exhibition was covered not only in the arts pages of the local press but also on the news and local affairs pages. In this way they were able to allow the work to function where it was of ultimate significance – in the real world, where real people go about their lives.

For some artists the street was the idealized working terrain for the visual arts in the 1970s. In 1972 at the Van Abbemuseum in Eindhoven, the then director Jean Leering even curated an exhibition entitled '*De Straat*' (The Street). And in the then still resolutely Social-Democratic city of Rotterdam – Tracy and Edwin's living and working environment for eight years – the notion of cultural participation had such currency that there was even a publicly-funded exhibition space in a shopping centre. Art was on the street, the threshold between art and reality was levelled and art became a participatory element in the process of creating the public's self-consciousness.

Mackenna and Janssen took to the streets in the 1990s not in order to raise public awareness or to realise a socialist dream. However, they did examine the possibilities of tackling real issues in a very real manner by incorporating their public's themes within the themes of their art. To follow on the heels of reality, to secure social solutions, to emphasise and concurrently deny art's artificial character, to bring art and experience closer together and to test the tenability of the experiential economy. All these ambitions and many others are also themes within the *white cube* of the museum, but in the reality of the street they appear all the more authentic. Furthermore, there is no object in the way, no artistic artefact between artist and public such as one normally finds (or at least expects to find, or indeed craves) in the museum. When talking of the direct relationship between artist, art work and the public, would not the manifestly physical work of art be a hindrance?

In Schiedam and also in Tokyo the street played an important role in their realisation of their vision. However, both projects were linked to art institutions – the Stedelijk Museum Schiedam and P3 Art and Environment Tokyo – and did not involve a denial of the significance of the aesthetic object. In both Schiedam and Tokyo there were clearly institutions that commissioned Mackenna and Janssen to research the relationship between the institution and the public. In Tokyo the most important part of the exhibition took place within the sheltered space of the institute itself.

P3 became a meeting place where the artists worked *live*; they moved their studio onto the project's doorstep. In presenting themselves so openly to the public they desecrated the aura of the *white cube*. The museum took on something of the studio and meeting place and the open studio took on something of the museum. The museum became the street and the street became the museum. The conversation in the open studio and in the museum formed an important constituent of the final art work that developed during the course of three weeks.

Processes and appliances

Tracy Mackenna and Edwin Janssen's work nearly always has a strong process-based character. That is expressed not only in a clear focus on direct contact with the public, but also in their interest in particular activities that circle around the production and proliferation of an object and which are firmly rooted in process. As the curator for their project for the group exhibition '*PEACE*' in the Migros Museum für Gegenwartskunst in Zurich (1999) I experienced at first hand the extent to which, for them, the process of making an object appears to be as important as the object itself. The production of a traditional blanket with a contemporary (visual) language was presented during the exhibition itself as a metaphor for the creative process.

I had previously observed Mackenna and Janssen at work

during the exhibition '*Go Away: Artists and Travel*' at the Royal College of Art in London. There too they sought direct contact with their public and confronted that public with its own (material) creative process. Indeed, even more than that: both in London and in Zurich the visitors' verbal and written contributions became the very material from which the blankets were made. In Zurich the visitors to the exhibition were able to communicate their ideas on the notion of peace to the artists or their stand-ins and so become direct participants in the process. Furthermore, the blanket's production process could be viewed on the internet allowing the same visitors to participate further.

The artistic process now takes place for a large part in the museum space itself, as is normally the case with a performance. But the process continues beyond the museum presentation. After the blanket has been physically produced in Orkney, incorporating all relevant quotes collected during the artists' meeting with the public, those contributors themselves have the opportunity to borrow the blanket for a while and use it at their discretion. Thus the creative process is still active after the exhibition and the object is not immediately institutionalised.

In this way Tracy and Edwin attempt to make performances that remain active for much longer than is normally the case. Just as the performances of many other relationists such as Rirkrit Tiravanija are no longer restricted to a relatively short and manageable presentation period, so Mackenna and Janssen's actions have little in common with the traditional performances from the early years of the medium. The performances of the relationist can last an entire exhibition, or even longer, and take on the form of installations. In recent years a new term has been coined for this form – the *performative installation*.

With their blanket projects Tracy Mackenna and Edwin Janssen managed to extend the shelf-life of their performances and their works and to increase the level of public participation. They attempted to create enduring objects that could guarantee a communicative and engaged relationship between artist and public.

With their blankets, which may be taken home and used for a limited period by participants, the artists pose important questions for these participants to consider. For, what exactly is this object that they have been allowed to take home? Is it a work of art? Following the Kantian formulation that a work of art is an object with no practical use, it seems that the blanket may not be defined as a work of art precisely because it can be used to keep oneself warm or to sleep beneath, thus making it difficult to deny its utility. In the domestic situation the blanket exists not only for its own sake but also indeed at the service of the household.

For some time our culture has been in a very fluid state in which the boundaries between various cultural manifestations appear to be obsolete. When performance art and theatre come together and when art, design and craft (blankets are a form of craft) come into contact within the artistic object, and the content is strongly determined by verbal elements, it has little sense to employ Kant's normative formulation as a definition. Mackenna and Janssen's performative installations are wonderfully fluid. Art enters into a dialogue with theatre, language, design and craft. Or maybe one should say that this art form is precisely the result of mobilising all these different elements, and all in the service of communicating with the public. Indeed, is not the union of these disciplines much better equipped to bring about an intense moment of identification between the artist and the public?

The discursiveness that lies within the association between the two artists, and which I earlier formulated as the most important potential of their collaboration, also appears to function within the fusion of these different disciplines. The media of the theatre and language strengthen the identification with the public and the interplay between art and craft extends the art form's communicative power and increases its recognisability for its *users*. Both the creative and communicative processes develop discursively.

Images

Discourse and process are also central to Mackenna and Janssen's more recent work. In 'Growth, Form and the Inevitability of Herself' the human process of growing older is compared with the growth cycles of a garden. In a pattern of eighteen video images, each individual image enters into a dialogue with the others. The work is like a contemporary still life composed of slow and subtle movements. Beauty and decay – classic themes from art history – coexist, and speak of the same development.

In their latest work Tracy Mackenna and Edwin Janssen appear to have chosen to consciously develop in the direction of a visual language that leaves behind the manifestly participatory element of their earlier work and to have exchanged it for a much more traditional medium – video. One can now say with some certainty that video has become *traditional* in recent decades. This urge comes partly from the desire to make work that is more personal and less dependent upon the public's input, which was not always able to deliver what the artists might have wanted.

Intimacy and the personal play an important role in the most recent work. The video installation 'Differences under the Skin' deals with Tracy's own Scots-Italian family and contains details of photographs taken by her father. The work was part of Mackenna and Janssen's exhibition at the CCA, which centred upon Scots identity; a public theme is given a *private* interpretation. The same is true of another new work in which a dead man talks about his euthanasia and his motives for ending his life. It is a confrontation between the private wish to die and public morals and legislation.

With this recent video work Tracy Mackenna and Edwin Janssen's art has become not only more personal and intimate but it also positions the artists in the midst of a process of reconsidering their visual values, which the relationists appear to have taken on board in recent years. With a growing scepticism of relationist art, under pressure from advancing neo-liberalist tendencies, there seems to have been a development towards incorporating other more traditional media and *languages* within this form of art. Although the activity of looking has gained greater importance in their work, it seems that the discursive element is still alive and well in Mackenna and Janssen's new projects. Not only is the continual tension between public and private still clearly present in their works, but so is the direct re-working of human norms and values, which has always formed a springboard for their direct communication with the public.

Together Tracy and Edwin work on art that can develop communication between the artists, the work of art and the public. Of the greatest importance in this respect is that the artistic duo is prepared to demonstrate the communicative qualities of their work even within their own creative methodology. In this way, the quality of their own communication is constantly tangible in the quality of their communication with their public. And that is, I would say, truly a *unique selling point*.

Rein Wolfs is Chief Curator at the Boijmans van Beuningen Museum in Rotterdam.

Until 2001 he worked as director at the Migros Museum für Gegenwartskunst in Zurich, which he created from the Migros Collection.

In the past Wolfs has curated solo exhibitions of the work of Alicia Framis, Rirkrit Tiravanija, Atelier van Lieshout and Douglas Gordon.

He has organised group exhibitions such as *Flexible* (1997), *ironisch/ironic* (1998) featuring, amongst others, Maurizio Cattelan, Steve McQueen and Aernout Mik; and *PEACE* (1999) which included Olaf Nicolai, Tracy Mackenna and Edwin Janssen, Bob & Roberta Smith and Piotr Uklanski.

Wolfs curated the Dutch contribution to the 50th International Art exhibition of *la Biennale di Venezia* (2003).

He is also the founding Publisher of '*Material, die Kunst-Illustrierte*', an art magazine in German.

THE JOHN & YOKO DRAWINGS

ACY MACKENNA
D EDWIN JANSSEN

WAR
IS
OVER!

IF YOU WANT IT

Love and Peace from ~~John & Yoko~~ Edwin & Tracy

WMD
ARE
THERE!
IF YOU WANT IT
Edwin & Tracy
Love and Peace from John & YoKo

A GRAVE NEW WORLD!
IF YOU WANT IT
Edwin&Tracy
Love and Peace from John&Yoko

LIFE IS OVER!
IF YOU WANT IT
Edwin & Tracy
Love and Peace from John & Yoko

DEATH
IS
GENTLE!
IF YOU WANT IT
Edwin & Tracy
Love and Peace from John & Yoko

GOD IS BACK!
IF YOU WANT IT
Edwin&Tracy
Love and Peace from John&Yoko

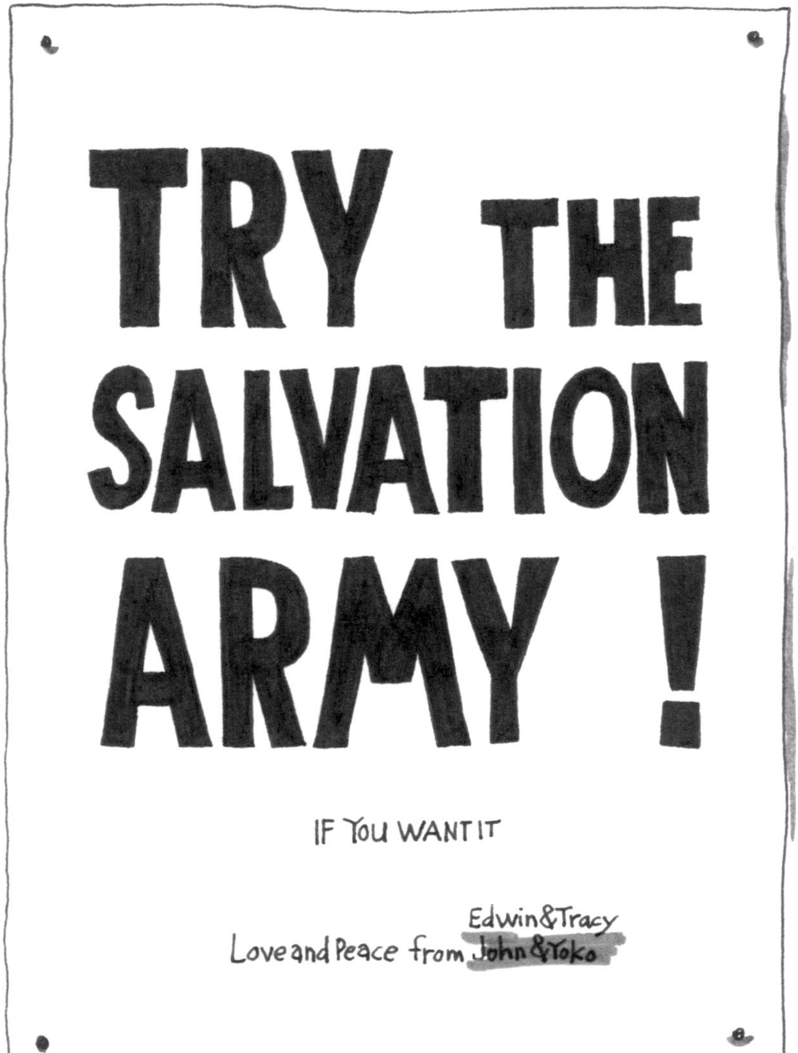
TRY THE SALVATION ARMY !
IF YOU WANT IT
Edwin&Tracy
Love and Peace from John&Yoko

THE JOHN & YOKO DRAWINGS, 2000 – ONGOING.

THE JOHN & YOKO DRAWINGS are part of an ongoing series of (wall) drawings based on a poster made by John Lennon & Yoko Ono for their peace campaign in the early seventies: 'WAR IS OVER! If you want it, Love and Peace from John and Yoko'. The drawings address a wide range of social, political and cultural issues. The first drawing in this series was made shortly after taking part in the exhibition 'Peace' curated by Rein Wolfs and Gianni Jetzer, Migros Museum für Gegenwartskunst Zurich, Switzerland, 1999-2000.

Secrets are safe with us

Secrets are safe with us

Listening is mixed up with identity. A small presence in a room, absorbing a language sellotaped together. Visibly eavesdropping, Italian clippings thrashing about in the musty air, colliding with tattered English, accumulating on the ground. The sounds are brown, the colour seeping across surfaces, suffusing the airwaves, language as dark as the house itself. Nonno the radio-controller is sitting, watching. Hair black, teeth broken, pipe smoking.

Invisible roots, negated to fit in. Differences under the skin, accommodated and accommodating. Temporary people, sitting on the surface, hankering for somewhere else. Rubbing away at the edges, sharpening their senses, confronting complacency. A margin lying as a strip, teetering near the brink. Replicating it now myself, a contemporary dilemma, tied to Scotland by work and family. Decide who you are.

Flakes of skin fall faster than particles of dust, both slow-motioned, decelerated by the voices pricking the air supply. Blown, bumped, displaced by breath, paths interrupted.

The clock in the pitch black hall ticking on. Holding back, watching, tracing Nonna's olivegreenandcream silk skirt against the cracked red leather of the couch. The same cracks that erode the Mull mountains, I slide off the glossy leather into the Atlantic.

The lines I made in the first place came from drawing with my fingers around the messages I wrote each winter in the condensation on the window pane, the transparency of the pale grey Atlantic ocean filling up the glass rectangle. My messages appeared and disappeared depending on the temperature inside and the external weather conditions. Sometimes one would be noticed months after it was written, sliding into view behind a head, instantly suspending conversation. It was at this point that I would slowly trace the snail-trail lines in between the letters and the words, marking out a giant invisible cobweb.

The letters varied greatly in size within a word, since when I wrote I focused on the sea behind and not on the window pane.

In the winter the white house was battered by storms spraying sea water, and seaweed clung in tatters to the harled outer walls, drying to a crisp as the weather turned slowly for the better. That part of the sea that came into contact with the bottom of the garden was in fact an open-ended channel, closed off at the front by the island of Kerrera. As we walked from room to room our movements were mimicked by those of the boats and ships that passed from left to right, or right to left, depending on whether they entered from the Sound of Mull or from the Sound of Kerrera. I saw either their arrival or their departure. Never both points on their journey.

Secrets are safe with us

Continual soakage, rivulets dribbling off the Mull mountains in Spring, the house built on a raised beach from the melting of a glacier. Wetness everywhere. Sloping down from the cliffs, draining back into the sea. I would stare for hours at the sea, standing in the pouring rain, silently silting over with salt, willing the waves' knife-edges to turn solid, slowly becoming cross-eyed. My love of salt comes from this gradual accumulation as it seeped into my clothes and hair and skin, and the salt soaked taste was reason enough to woo innocent boyfriends down to the rocks, just to be able to lick that taste from them.

An SNP badge on my mossy green jumper. Worn for dad with a tinge of shame.

Messages carried from country to country, by word of mouth. Laboriously scrawled, lead streaking the single lined page. Long periods of time away from home, unable on your return to tell your story. Language Limbo Land. Mono-cultural Scotland harbouring mono-cultural Italians. Insisting on my language with Erasmus, not allowing what was done to mum and to me to be done to him in turn. Erasmus' words come staggering out, the city formed the first of them, car auto car auto.

Window hanging, watching the world from his 50's turret. Eye level with the birds and their failing nest, the closest he gets to animals. Watching, from inside. The urge to be out has him clawing at the door, writhing on the doormat, desperate for nature where the woods are freedom and he knows no rules. The flat restricts him, searching for something he cannot find. In town, his trees are dog toilets that he mustn't go near.

I am claimed by the Collemacchiese and the Gaels. Amalia's grand-daughter, revealed by my looks. In Ireland I am also a daughter of the Spanish West Coast, in Romania, a gypsy, in Buenos Aires, an Italian. I can't hide.

From the cliff above, looking down on The Lodge, yolk-yellow spores growing circular on the white harling, the sea's virus. Lying undetected in a home-made nest of bracken. Clouds passing, rain melting, wind whistling. Ant-like below, my beloved family, wholly unaware.

Two tiny explorers in Collemacchia, staking our mother's claim in a makeshift tent on our grandmother's loggia. A protest at bread and tomatoes. Nonna's favourite figs on the loggia she no longer used, eaten alone with Ronald, tasted for the first time without mum and dad, eaten until we puked. Wine with a wee bit of water, enough to make us weird, different from our friends. Nonno's peaches, fur in my hands in a steaming Glasgow greenhouse, the house itself icing over from the inside. Water sliding over gloss paint kitchen walls. Lying in bed, mouth and nostrils steaming, afraid to move for fear of losing heat.

Watching tourists watching sunsets, sucking Scotland in, silenced by nature. Basking in the heat of the settling sun filtered by their cardboard-cut-out-bodies. The lapping sea an unstable ground, the sunset the ceiling over their heads. Tilt your head backwards and look at the sky.

Red wellies in the lemon meringue pie.

Filignano - Glasgow - Oban - Glasgow - Filignano - Glasgow - Oban
- Glasgow - Filignano.

Food wrapped in newspaper brought by bus by Nonna to Oban.
Fried chicken flattened in the pan, syrupy meat, pepperonata in sweet
vinegar, frittata at Easter, shoosh from the leftover pizza dough. The
same house 40 years on. Meals at mum's. Different food, corrupted
cooking. Slowness of preparation, speed of consumption. Erasmus
balancing on my shoulder, yelling at the wall, his back to the gathering.

I am a lover of Nature. Seeping through my pores, influencing my choices, I rejected then returned. Elevating, relieving, breath-giving-oxygenating, safe, silent and constant.

(Or just a Victorian fantasy.) The garden is an extension of the house, ours a world with children's codes. Outside is thinking space. Peasant Molise in urban Glasgow.

Secrets are safe with us

Secrets are safe with us

TRACY MACKENNA
AND EDWIN JANSSEN

A PERFECT
IMAGE OF
OURSELVES

CENTRE FOR CONTEMPORARY ARTS / GLASGOW

ED AND ELLIS
N SCHIEDAM

ED AND ELLIS IN SCHIEDAM

Stedelijk Museum Schiedam and the streets
of Schiedam, the Netherlands, 1998.

Asked by the museum to look at its
relationship with its audience, we embarked
on a prolonged period of research into the
history and contemporary aspirations of the
town. With access to City Council reports
where the future of Schiedam was debated,
the idea developed of using the forthcoming
local elections to examine the identity
crisis faced by the city. The fake political
party List 0* was established, and the actor
John Buysman commissioned to play party
leader Koos van der Sluis. He took to the
streets to bring List O to the attention of the
Schiedammers with us as his promotional
team distributing flyers, folders and balloons
- No crap! List O!

Almost everyone has something to say about
politics even if they don't use their right
to vote. Many of the people on the streets
expressed their frustration with politics
and politicans. Realising that we were
campaigning for a fake party they dropped
their defences and said they would have
voted for List O, assuming we would be a
'protest party', taking the piss out of local
politics. By presenting an approach to art that
was unfamiliar in the area it was possible to
show the museum that they could make new
connections to the world beyond.

The related film documented the candidate's
campaign and life and was shown on
national television during the official election
campaign. Filming took place while the other
political parties were canvassing, one local
party candidate demanding live on radio
the nullification of the campaign results. He
objected to his party's posters being covered
by those of List 0. 'Free entry, free coffee'
- the shopping public was stimulated to visit
the museum where one gallery was set up
as a campaign headquarters, showing the
documentary about Koos van der Sluis and
List 0. The museum staff that made up Koos'
band practised daily on a podium.

*In the Netherlands a list number represents each
political party. The lower the number, the more electe
seats the party has.

STICKERS /
POSTERS

MUPPIES

Limited Interest
① PUBLICA

T-SHIRTS / PRINTED STUFF
SUIT — PLACARD

PLACARD

② PUBLICATIE — DOCUMENTATIE

POSTER — always appearin
in photos of diff
locations in
schiedam

GEZOCHT
(MENEER)
SCHIEDAM

LIJST 0

racy Mackenna
Edwin Janssen
Ed en Ellis
n Schiedam

edelijk Museum Schiedam
27 februari - 19 april 1998

INTERVIEWS

SELECT
which parties
which people

QUESTIONS

LOCATIONS — in Schiedam

film in
AUTO
/ CAR

turn into
promo video for
LITST O — snappy,

Formulate
our concept
of Schiedam

declare no
position

show video
MUS

s.o present to ta
to visitors

DOCUMENTATION of WHAT WE DO ON STREE

WE ARE

I'M READY
TO JUMP
INTO YOUR
OPEN MIND

Font:
VALKEN

WE ARE READY
TO JUMP INTO
YOUR
OPEN MIND

← Ed and Ellis in

ED AND ELLIS
N TOKYO

ED AND ELLIS IN TOKYO
P3 Art and Environment, Tokyo Metropolitan Museum of Contemporary Art, Nadiff Gallery and the streets of Tokyo, Japan, 1998.

P3 art and environment supports its art projects through its activities in urban planning. At the time, this was unique in Tokyo where the dominance of the commercial system meant that artists hired galleries to put on their exhibitions.

Tokyo had been undergoing change partly due to a series of economic crises that caused a shift in the way that the city's inhabitants saw their futures and the future of the city. Uncertainty and insecurity had pervaded the lives of particularly younger Japanese people. P3 invited us to look at their organisation's role in relation to the changing needs of its audience.

In the research phase of the project, we took part in architecture, art and design workshops in Tokyo with the aim of meeting groups who were analysing contemporary issues related to living in Tokyo. Through this interaction we began to develop the project that would focus on these issues within a purpose-built environment that used P3's gallery space as the centre, with satellite venues. A range of inter-related events responded to expressions of alienation amongst particularly the 18-35 year olds from their peer group and from their elders. People wanted to engage with the city's development in order to understand individual experiences such as belonging, attachment and memory. Tokyo's cultural, social and architectural systems were described as alienating rather than inclusive. This, together with a new lack of trust in what had been a traditionally secure future resulted in feelings of anxiety. These fears were compounded by the fact that as Japanese they had not been educated to think creatively about solutions and alternatives.

In the developmental stages of the project, P3 transformed its way of working by integrating itself, the audience, public space, other venues and us. It brought together organisations that would not normally have worked together and dissolved the usual distinctions between exhibition, public art and community art practice.

In *Ed and Ellis in Tokyo* we set up the first

in a series of purpose-built public studios. Central to the project was a wool blanket that each day incorporated extracts of conversations between visitors and us about their lives in Tokyo and their aspirations for Japanese society and themselves as individuals. The gallery was transformed into a public meeting place and was quickly adopted as a regular venue. A lecture programme highlighted issues such as architecture's effect on collective memory and the (im)probability of integration into Japanese society by other Asian cultures. The café that became part of the temporary exhibition space functioned as a creative zone for invited DJ's each of whom was involved in a specific area of visual practice. The project was made possible by the participation of the 12 volunteers recruited by P3. They acted as hosts, interpreters and translators in the museum and accompanied us onto the streets as a promotional team while we distributed promotional material, mimicking Tokyo street advertising strategies. The three satellite venues hosted elements of the project including public lectures and a bus tour of Tokyo's motorway network.

P3 art and environment proposed to adopt the satellite venue structure developed in our project as a way forward for their organisation, evolving a new working mode and a new approach to the use of their exhibition space. Co-ordinated by P3, *Ed and Ellis in Tokyo*'s network continued as the blanket, after machining in Scotland, was given to the people whose texts were incorporated in it, to use as they wanted.

The experience of devising and working on the project was exceptional for us. The openness and the desire to engage encountered in the people we worked with and the audience was overwhelming. The lack of cynicism that distinguishes the Japanese art audience from a European audience reinforced for us art's ability to have an immediate and direct impact, and that it can in fact affect people's lives in a lasting way.

As in many of our projects there were t-shirts flyers, fold-outs, stickers and balloons that were given away in exchange for conversation and as promotional material. Designed in collaboration with Stout/Kramer this was the beginning of a long-term relationship with the Dutch designers.

Saturday 18 October

started at Nadiff
50 + people
'Ed + Ellis in Tokyo Bus Tour' sign on fron
over expressways MEX (have map – can
make
Bento box lunch standing in car park
– arm extension of expressway.
our Talk at MOT — more than the 50 pe
↓
we stood for 2 hours
showing slides + answe

(almost)
Everyone w
COMMUNICAT
suggested we
— WHY DO THE J
— or Communi
— because the
— another form
— is INTER – Co
communicati

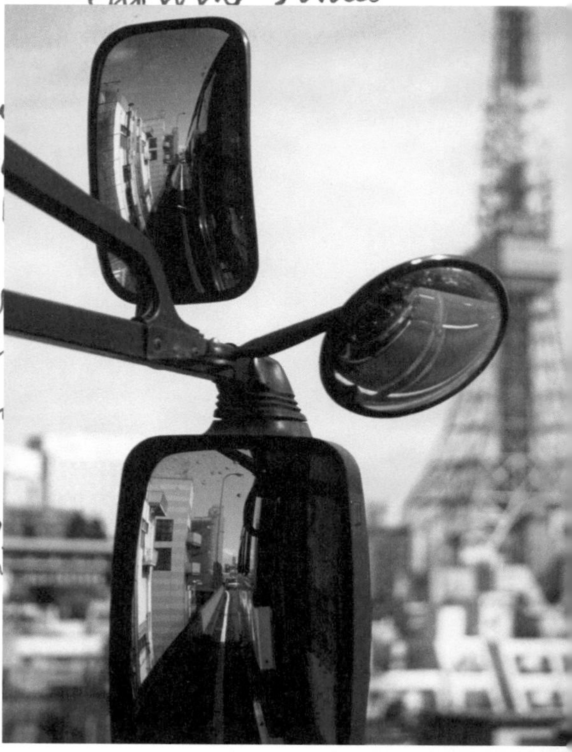

PLEASE ENJOY
A FINE SELECTION
OF MATERIAL
WHICH ARE
    LUXURIOUS AND
  DELICIOUS

Tuesday 20 October   11⁰⁰ — Ernesto at Dutch Embassy

WHAT'S THE IMAGE OF TOKYO ABROAD

blackboard question

Our impressions in Tok

LONELINESS
ONENESS
SADNESS
CONFUSION
VULNERABLE

in P3 today
gallery
cutting these words

FEAR of MISTAKES

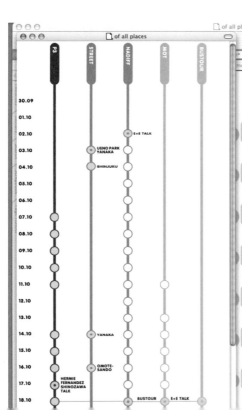

of all places / Tracy Mackenna & Edwin Janssen

Mac OS X   Microsoft MacTopia

of all places

	P3	STREET	NADIFF	MOT	BUSTOUR
30.09					
01.10					
02.10			E+E TALK		
03.10		UENO PARK YANAKA			
04.10		SHINJUKU			
05.10					
06.10					
07.10					
08.10					
09.10					
10.10					
11.10					
12.10					
13.10					
14.10		YANAKA			
15.10					
16.10		OMOTE-SANDO			
17.10	HERMIE FERNANDEZ SHINOZAWA TALK				
18.10			BUSTOUR	E+E TALK	

kyo Ed & Ellis in T
kyo Ed & Ellis in T
kyo Ed & Ellis in T
kyo Ed & Ellis in T
kyo Ed & Ellis in T
kyo Ed & Ellis in T
kyo Ed & Ellis in T
kyo Ed & Ellis in T

FEAR OF MAKING MISTAKES

Groups of 50+ year old women = Pronto

- no fussed - all talk so loudly

- difficult age - nightmare looming

Japanese

- convenient
- contradictions
- oneness
- cigarette smoke
- loneliness
- confusion

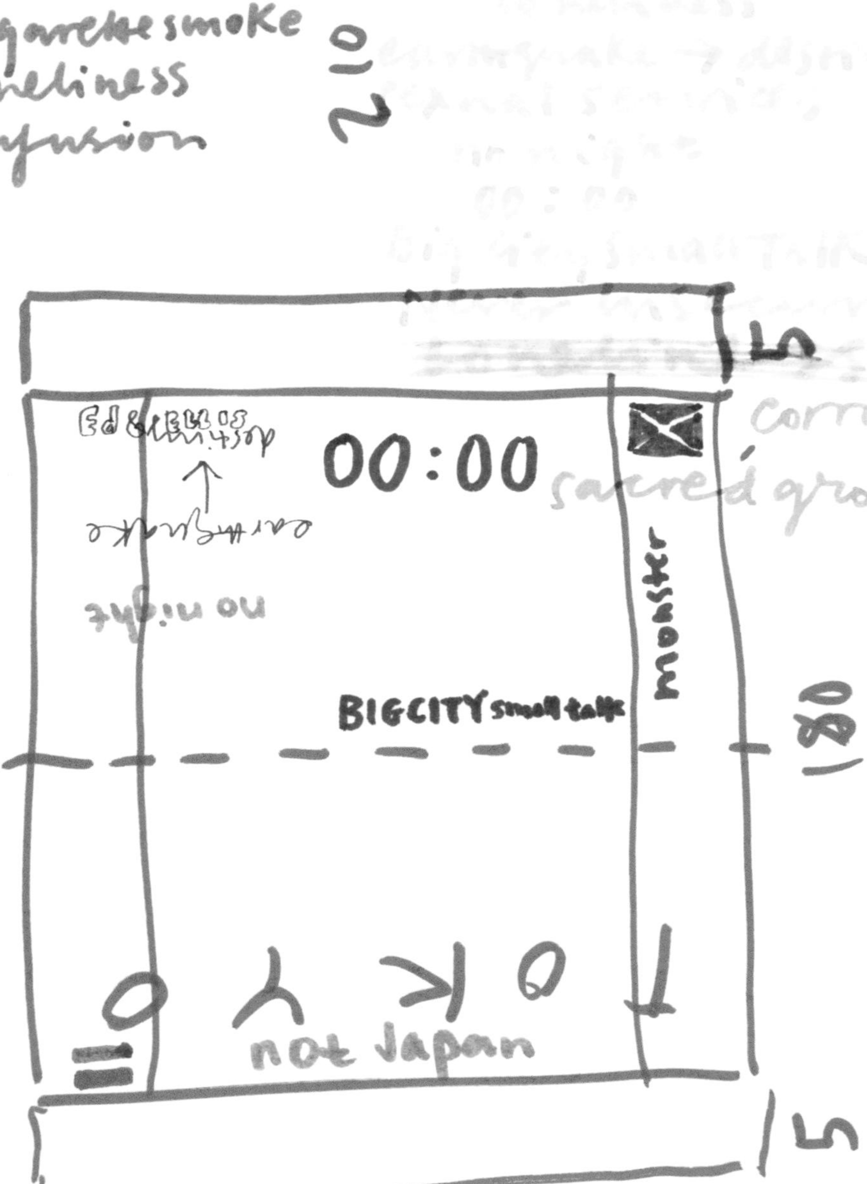

012

Ed&...

↑ oshimako

earthquake

no night

00:00

corrup-

sacred ground

monster

BIGCITY small talk

180

not Japan

5

5

day 22 october

interviewed by 'the English Journal' by a
Canadian journalist who was en route to
France ... ended up staying 5 years so far.
What would you miss....?' — SUSHI

- Talk series _____   Kisei Kobayashi
                              ↓
                        book: Mechanised Tokyo

- showed slides without talking
- then responded to questions.

coming clearer to us that our project offers
ost unique opportunity for japanese people to
foreigners in relaxed atmosphere — informal.

oming back to question:
at is it the japanese want out of 'communication'.

KYO IS A WAITING ROOM

- almost last train
  Yotsua-Sanchome Stn — skinny businessman in
typical pale grey suit + briefcase, totally legless on platform
pposite us — his train comes, goes — he's still on platform
uckled up. How will he get home? Will he be thrown on
or put outside when station closes?

P3 gallery
↓
construction - more worried

17³⁰ — Tim
        Daily Yomiuri

THE DISEASE of LOSING MEMORIES

TOKYO'S LOSING ITS MEMORY

When the buildings go, it's hard to keep hold of
the memories without visual triggers
— copying buildings from Europe transfers memory
                                    from the copy

pm / went to Shin-okubo
      low prices advertised in windows
      cheap sushi train ↓ ¥130

supposedly where first non-japanese communities
    settled (other asians)

PUT MY NAME
ON EVERYTHING

I PUT MY NAME ON EVERYTHING
Tron Theatre, Glasgow, Scotland, 1998.

During the re-build of the Tron Theatre complex we requested that we be based in the staff's temporary offices in a nearby street overlooking the theatre.

The desk we used in the large open-plan office situated us in the midst of the theatre's business. This allowed us to talk to staff about the theatre and to see how they worked at their jobs and with each other, and to talk about our role as artists. Discussing the roles of staff and staff interaction was not our original intention, but quickly became fascinating as our roles as artists took on a function within the office space. A process of exchange took place where we were expected to transform information into something that would be of benefit to this specific group of people. Accepting us into their working environment, staff discussed with us our role in the rebuilding of their theatre. They expressed their feelings of alienation from what they had anticipated as a consultation process and as a development of the ethos of a small artist-initiated theatre.

Conversations moved towards issues surrounding the creation and occupation of an ideal work environment, professional relationships, territory and the balance between private and working lives.

As relationships developed with the staff, we shifted from the idea of making a work for the public areas of the theatre to making a work for their offices. The final phase of development, the furnishing of the offices, was to be severely limited in terms of funding. An award-winning building housed age-old furniture and equipment.

The outcome of this consultation process was a wool carpet containing anonymous quotes from a series of interviews with the staff that worked for the Tron during the period of the rebuild. The carpet is a collective portrait of that particular group of people, installed in their offices on two floors of the new Tron Theatre.

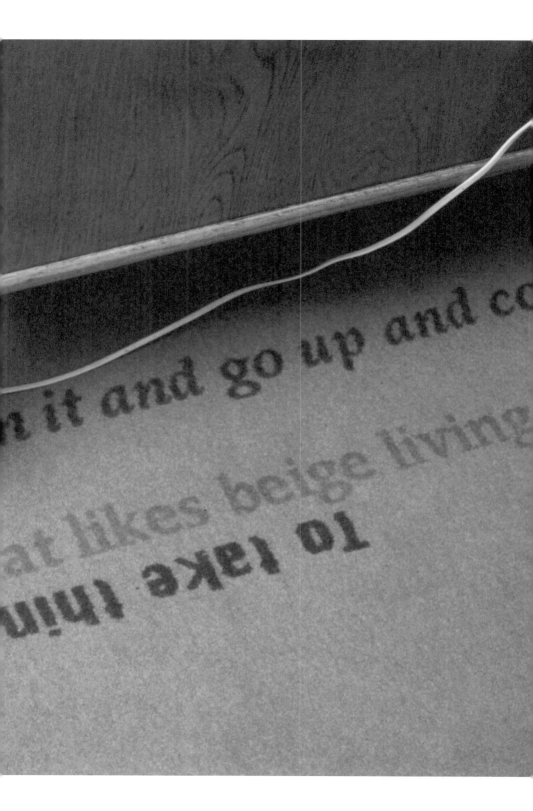

'Being good at my job
is more important to
me than being a good
colleague'

I need to k

'I will be very welcoming to people but it will be my space'

'I know that I am a territorial person'

ED AND ELLIS
IN EVER EVER LAND

ED AND ELLIS IN EVER EVER LAND
CCA, Centre for Contemporary Arts,
Glasgow, Scotland, 2001.

For CCA's reopening we were invited to
develop work that focussed on Scottish
identity. The research period coincided
with the opening of the Scottish
parliament, when some were of the opinion that its
establishment arose out of a sense of cultural
difference rather than a drive for political
change.

The research period revealed how
difficult it was to get to grips with Scotland's
identity. The many faces presented were
a combination of the legacy of generations
of myth making and the overwhelming
visual imagery of tartan and shortbread.
For all the heroism, identity seemed to be
reinvented on a daily basis, the bravura and
insecurities those of a young adolescent.
As Kevin Toolis wrote in the Guardian
Weekend in 1999, 'Truth and lies are
interchangeable when it comes to national
myths' and he continued 'anything – past,
present or future – can be manipulated for
a nationalist agenda.'* It was remarkable to
see how Scottish national identity continues
to be defined in relation to England; almost
300 years after Scotland and England formed
the Union that created Britain.

We travelled and filmed extensively, talking
to people about their opinions on Scots
identity and their ideas for the future of
the country. The enormous differences
between our respective homelands
became a significant issue. The Scots were
characterised as lacking self-confidence
and expressing a desire to recreate and relive
the past when asked to imagine the future.
The Dutch by contrast were characterised as
overly self aware, a nation that trivialises its
cultural heritage in favour of an almost
zealous commitment to the future.

Our presentation consisted of three
elements:

A series of eight printed envelopes was
produced in collaboration with graphic
designers Stout/Kramer. Each envelope
contained a printed insert that showed
elements of the visual research process.
One insert was the text *Secrets are safe
with us*, which is reprinted in this book.

The video installation *Differences under
the skin* deals with more personal subject
matter. The work looks at the integration
into Scotland of Tracy's Italian family. It is
partly based on her Scottish father's slides
that document family members affected by
emigration from Italy and the Scots Italians
who are the result of that emigration.

In the gallery we worked on a text blanket,
gathering opinions and statements about
Scotland and Scottishness through
conversation with visitors and from written
contributions left on a large pin board.
A recurring element of the blanket projects i
their use by the people who have contribute
to the making process. A daily website
update tracked the blanket's progress.

* 'Scotland, the Vainglorious', Kevin Toolis, Guardian
Weekend, April 24, 1999.

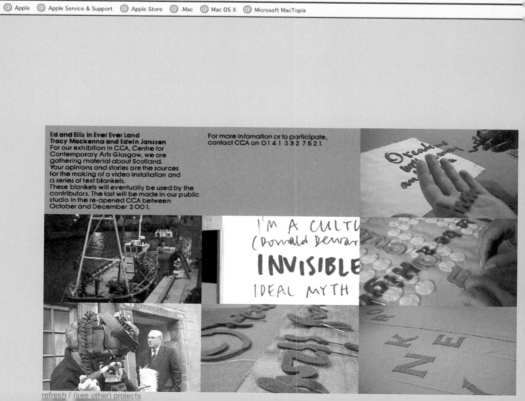

@ Apple   @ Apple Service & Support   @ Apple Store   @ .Mac   @ Mac OS X   @ Microsoft MacTopia

Ed and Ellis in Ever Ever Land
Tracy Mackenna and Edwin Janssen
For our exhibition in CCA, Centre for
Contemporary Arts Glasgow, we are
gathering material about Scotland.
Your opinions and stories are the sources
for the making of a video installation and
a series of text blankets.
These blankets will eventually be used by the
contributors. The last will be made in our public
studio in the re-opened CCA between
October and December 2001.

For more infomation or to participate,
contact CCA on 0141 332 7521.

I'M A CULT
(Donald Dewar

INVISIBLE

IDEAL MYTH

refresh / (see other) projects

...cation text → say sth. about text ?
blankets.

a range of individuals' stories

...ly / or different?

working

TOWN, CITY, REGION, COUNTRY

develops through contact with
public

our presence ——→ on streets
in making of film
installation CCA
documentary publication
blankets

STRUCTU

EVER EVER LAND

invisible ——→ VISIBLE
VISUAL

+

show on
developi
reflect
on Scot

participatory {contribute
+ intervene

series of small publications
website

our travels through Scotland — talking to people / filmin
gathering opinions

audience / public ↔ ED AND ELLIS → CCA

Dutch / Scottish
2 differing perspectives

stimulate
these relationships

vital
but not good
in itself

Structures
generate
communications
participation

conversation

resulting networks
maintained by projects'
participants after we leave

blankets

social + politi...

art co...

EVER
EVER
LAND

d the vainglorious

np of the United Kingdom / political death of
                                    the United Kingdom

political Scottishness

nt to deconstruct the current British State"
ngo MacDonald, SNP **CULTURAL NATIONALIST**
uld not deny the charge of being a cultural
alist. I am proud of Scotland's contribution.
o protest against this political nationalism +
er arrogant view that, because I do not go
st mile with them, then in some sort of way
and I have actually been called this –
mig' and 'a traitor'. "
nald Dewar, First Minister for Scotland

IS SCOTTISHNESS ?   How does it differ from
                     Englishness, or political
                     Unionism?

ising of what the SNP calls its "INVISIBLE
                                 NATION "

une 1999
guration of the Scottish Youth Parliament

                    children of Scotland playing
                    visible role in 1 July proceedings

iament has its full powers from point
ween meets with it, although it has been
y for past couple of months.

THE FUTURE:

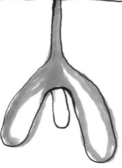

PROUD TO BE A HIGHLANDER

SCOT

BRITISH

EUROPEAN

Charles
Kennedy, inaugural speech, liberal leader 23 Sept 99

IT'S PATRIOTIC TO BE EUROPEAN

DIFFERENCES
UNDER THE SKIN

DIFFERENCES UNDER THE SKIN
CCA, Centre for Contemporary Art, Glasgow,
Scotland, 2001.

Differences under the skin is the first in a
series of video installations that address
personal subjects. About the integration into
Scotland of Tracy's mother's Italian family,
it is largely based on the slides made by
her Scottish father. His images are of family
members, Italians affected by emigration
from the Molise region of Italy, both through
leaving or having been left and the Scots
Italians who are the result of that emigration.
Migration from Italy to Scotland was part
of the larger Italian economic emigration
that started in the 18th century. The Molise
region is a mountainous and impenetrable
landscape, an underdeveloped area of small
towns and villages. Due to the high
percentage of emigration from the region,
the regional government has recently
adopted policies that examine cultural and
identity issues in people from Molise living
abroad. This is in response to requests
from emigrants to strengthen their contacts
with the region and is significant given the
marked increase in the phenomenon of
return emigration.

The images that Tracy's father made record
the complex process of assimilation into a
new culture over a number of generations.

The people, personal effects, interiors,
significant places, religious feasts and
festivals, the portrait and location
photographs give clues as to how the
Italians established themselves in their new
surroundings. What is also revealed is to
what degree Italian identity was stimulated
or enhanced, how cultural continuity was
maintained through beliefs, values, customs,
language and traditions and the importance
of the home and objects, personal
belongings, décor and place in terms of
leave-taking and assimilation.

New images made by us document many
of the people in Tracy's father's images and
record new family members.

18 simultaneously moving images in grid
format scrutinise in extreme close-up the
original images. The slow, hypnotic pace and
the large-scale of the projection causes the
viewer to constantly seek new combinations
and groupings of images.

This work is dedicated to Ronald G Mackenna.

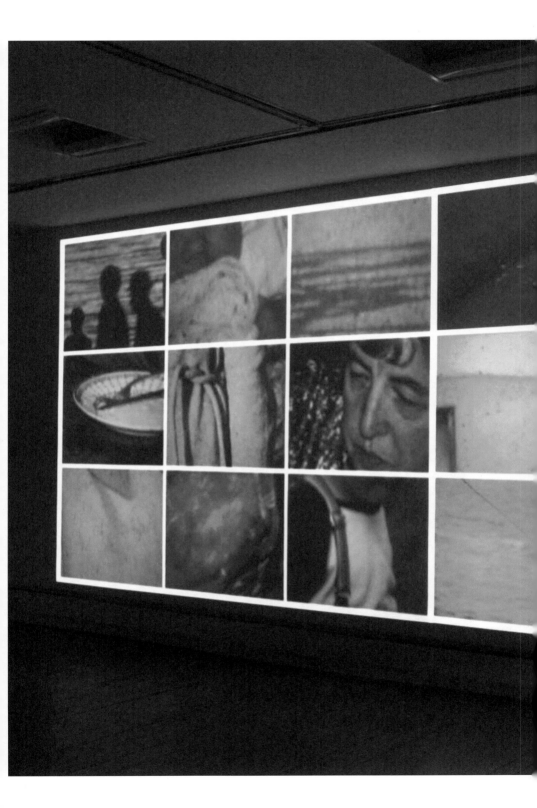

WAR IS OVER!

WAR IS OVER!
Part of the exhibition Peace, Migros Museum für Gegenwartskunst Zurich, Switzerland, 1999-2000.

In 1999 we were invited by Rein Wolfs to take part in *Peace*, an exhibition that looked at contemporary ideas of peace. During the course of the exhibition we made one of our blankets. It started as a blank surface onto which comments and extracts of conversations with visitors about the idea of peace today were stitched. At the end of the project the blanket was used by the people whose contributions were included in it and finally became part of the Migros Museum collection.

Due to the birth of our son Erasmus we couldn't be present all the time and so the large black and white photo of us as John and Yoko became our surrogate. Also shown was a poster based on the poster John Lennon & Yoko Ono produced for their peace campaign in the early seventies: WAR IS OVER! If you want it, Love and Peace from John and Yoko. John & Yoko's campaign for world peace was

not only an expression of real social and political concern but is also an early and good example of public art. Full of utopian naïvety and self-promotion, it didn't bring world peace but the photographs of John & Yoko in bed made it into our history books. As Gavin Brown said in the *Peace* exhibition catalogue 'Of any contemporary figure no one is more identified in the public mind with vague notions of peace than John Lennon'. In 2000, the year of the Zurich project, these nostalgic images had no relationship with actual political reality. A call for peace was a meaningless gesture from the past. There was no global peace movement and the many regional wars had virtually no impact on our lives in the so-called West. September 11th changed all that and when the wars in Afghanistan and Iraq were fought, a peace movement rose from it's grave.

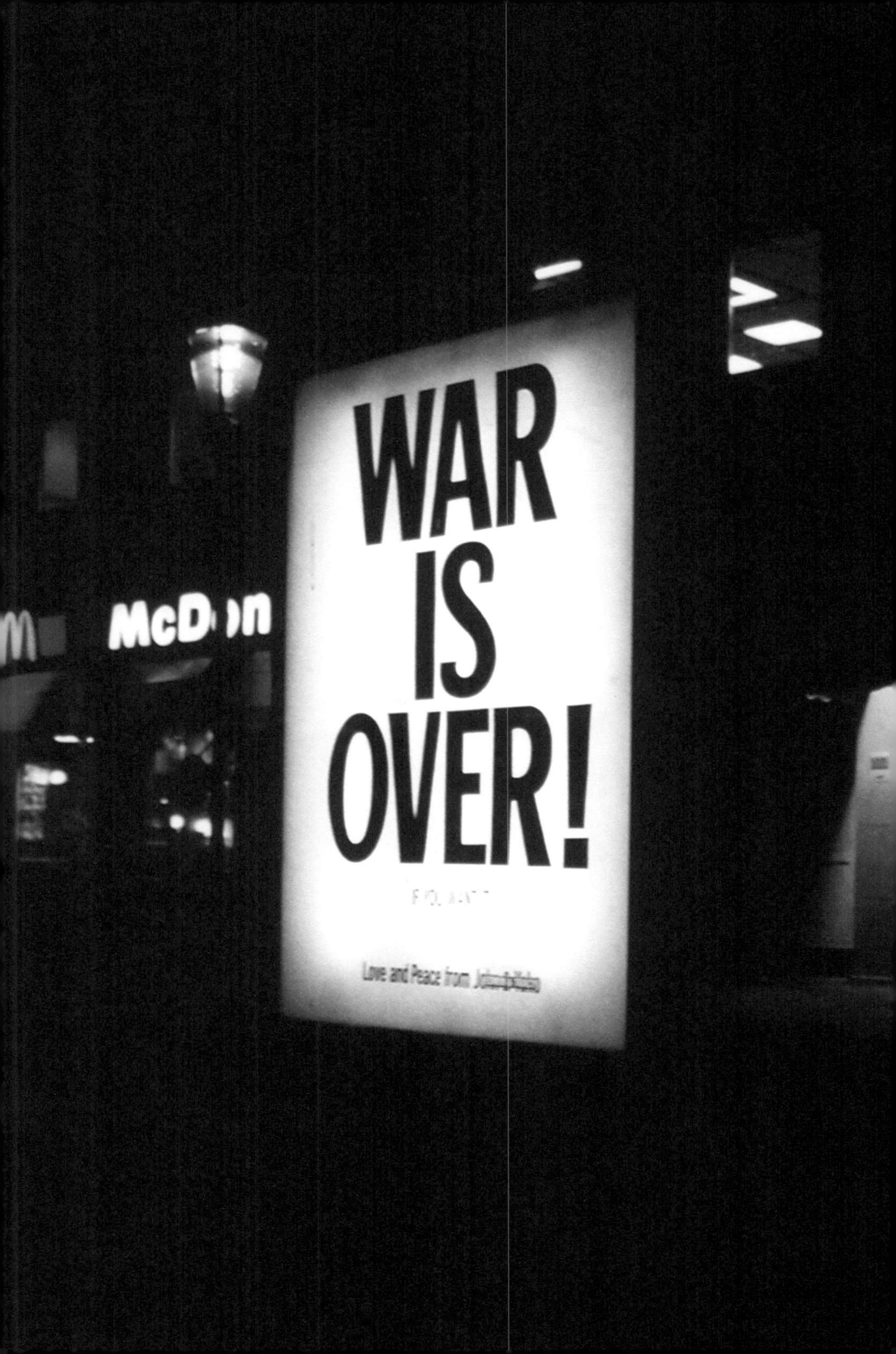
WAR
IS
OVER!
Love and Peace from

WAR IS OVER!

IF YOU WANT IT

Love and Peace from Edwin & Tracy ~~John & Yoko~~

GROWTH, FORM AND THE INEVITABILITY OF HERSELF

GROWTH, FORM AND THE INEVITABILITY
OF HERSELF
Centre d'Arts Plastiques et Visuels, Lille,
France, 2004.

In 2002 we moved from Rotterdam to
semi-rural Scotland, from a flat in the
centre of a dynamic city that has undergone
continuous rebuilding since the bombing
suffered in the second world war, to a house
with a garden in a tiny village between two
large cities. The partly abandoned garden
that we took on re-activated interests in
cultivated nature, land ownership and
cycles of growth and decay.

In *Growth, form and the inevitability of
herself*, the growth cycle of a garden is
shown in relation to the human process
of ageing. The development of the work
coincided with the planning of the
Merchant's House garden in Kirkcaldy,
Scotland. The abandoned site is a former
riggs garden attached to the mainly
17th century house of former merchants
who traded from the east coast with the
Baltic states and the Netherlands.

The video work questions accepted notions
of beauty as close-ups of decaying matter
become images of striking beauty.
The progressive stages of ageing in one
woman's life are juxtaposed with detail of
plant matter and art historical references.
The work is a contemporary still life,
nature morte informed by the 17th century
Dutch tradition. The extreme close-ups
prohibit an instant understanding of any
one full image. Eighteen images move
hypnotically and independently of each
other in a grid pattern across a large area.

Commissioned by CCA for the centenary celebrations
of the Entente Cordiale.

text

THE BREMEN COLLECTION 2003

THE BREMEN COLLECTION 2003
Part of *No Man is an Island*.
Various locations in Bremen and Gesellschaft
für Aktuelle Kunst, Bremen, Germany, 2003.

The way we start in a new place is often in
the role of a tourist. Gradually we gather
information around a specific area of interest,
and access and contribute to particular kinds
of knowledge through research trips that
involve meeting people and mapping the
city or area, walking, filming, writing,
drawing, talking. What remains constant
in each project is that we are aware of our
status as visitors, and have no pretentions
otherwise. This position has a positive
effect, allowing people to open-up in the
knowledge that we will eventually leave.

No Man is an Island, curated by Horst Griese
and Eva Schmidt, gave us the opportunity
to design and print fabrics for a series of
clothes commenting on Bremen. Research
focused on the history of fashion and an
exploration of Bremen's past as a Hanseatic
trading city and its multiethnic present
and contemporary activity as a centre for
aeronautics and space travel industry.
The problem that we faced was in how to
bring together the past, something defined
and definable, and the future, something
that the city was attempting to define.
The city's history was visible, documented
in image and text and as anecdote and story.
As is the case in many cities with an influen-
tial history, in direct contrast to the secured
image of the past, the city's future is often
a fluid entity, a series of projected ideas that

do not grow organically but are the result
of a political and economic need to define
a new image. Our aim was to make a work
that brought past, present and future
together. The audience for the work would
be Bremen's citizens, and so the work
was put back into the city as a catalyst for
conversation, comment and discussion.

The wearers of the six outfits became the
vehicles that enabled dissemination, the
clothes worn in the city during a series
of unscheduled appearances. The lack of
announcements and the casual air that
the wearers adopted allowed them to
mingle with the public, the absence of
an advertising or marketing strategy
making them non-confrontational.

During the research phase we looked at
how the city markets itself. The sometimes
uneasy juxtaposition of garments in some of
the outfits created an immediate feeling of
the clothes not belonging to a label or brand
thereby not having a single 'message' to im
part. The Zükunft Soldat as an example, was
confrontational in its direct reference to
the city's political past, reinforced by the
oddity of the half-man, half-boy sizing.

Portraiture is a recurring component of our
work, and with these clothes we consciously
set out to make a contemporary portrait of
the city. The portrait was activated when all
outfits were worn together and subject to the
influence of the individual wearers.

The model combines a knee-length, box-pleated skirt and a blouse with a large, rounded collar, gathered sleeves and oversized cuffs fastened by covered buttons. The repeating filigree pattern of the skirt in red and white, and the starkly contrasting blue, purple and white, large checked pattern of the blouse form a disparate whole. The pattern of the skirt material is created by combining an image of the Bremen town musicians, stylised to a silhouette, and a portrait of the female poisoner, Gesche Gottfried. The cuffs of the blouse are entirely covered with brightly-coloured photographs of displays in souvenir shops.

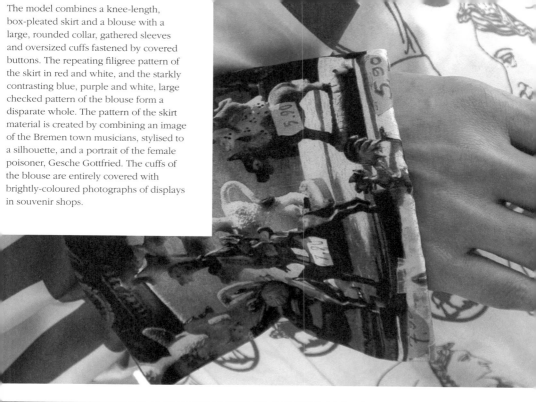

On completed dress:

poss. sprayed (stencilled) text.

cover buttons. poss. with Becks logo?

with shawl/scarf - photographic image.
trade

include outfit:

Outfit M

This simple, figure-hugging dress is made of jute, the same material as the coffee sacks which were individually handled for a long time at the docks. It is, of course, a reference to the history of Bremen as a trade city belonging to the Hansa League. The model is based on a design in the "New look" by Christian Dior (Day Dress, autumn/winter 1957). The wide, bell-shaped, swinging skirt is gathered at the waist, the top is finished with a large round collar. The red-brown woven border of the length of jute was used to finish the sleeves and the skirt's hem. The covered buttons show a depiction of a Hansa cog, reproduced in a porcelain painting from the 18th century that is now displayed in the Focke Museum. (Inscription on the original: De Christiani of Bremen, Capt. Blas Sager.)

The khaki coloured shirt worn by the model is assembled from two different halves; one half appears to be too small for the wearer, the other too big. He has obviously grown out of one part, but cannot yet fill out the other completely. A pair of knee-length blac trousers and knee-socks complete the outfit. Their design is based on the uniform of the Hitler Youth in Bremen. A sew-on label "Fut Soldier" decorates the shirt breast, on the sleeve we see the emblem of the youth secti "Gorch Fock". A scarf wound around the wearer's neck cites a line from one of its son "We are the soldiers of the future, bearers of deeds to come."

luorescent strips — moon
print

s.

it your planes, the girl said.
megas?.   FIND.

apron — moon
tabs — fl

enough
silver ma
_____
moon-print a
- details n
decide

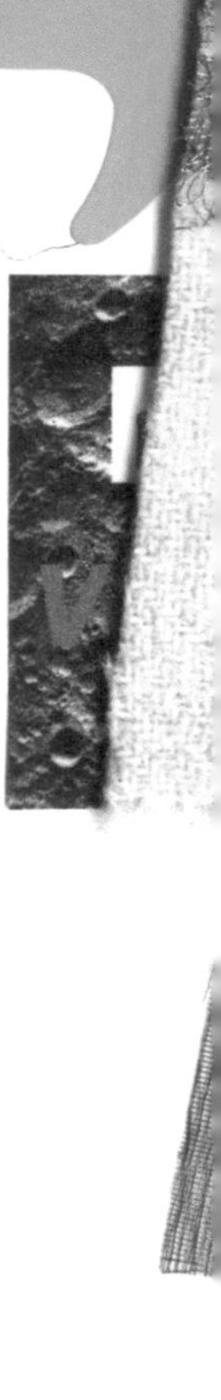

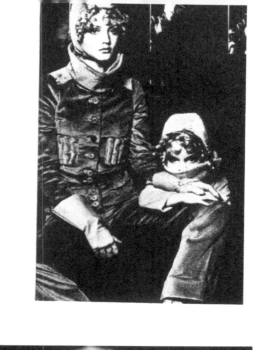

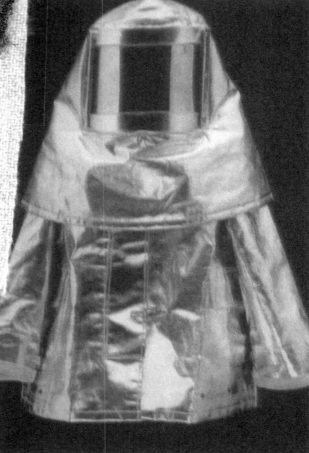

Single
Punched

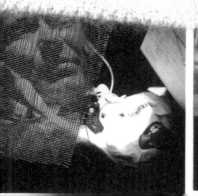

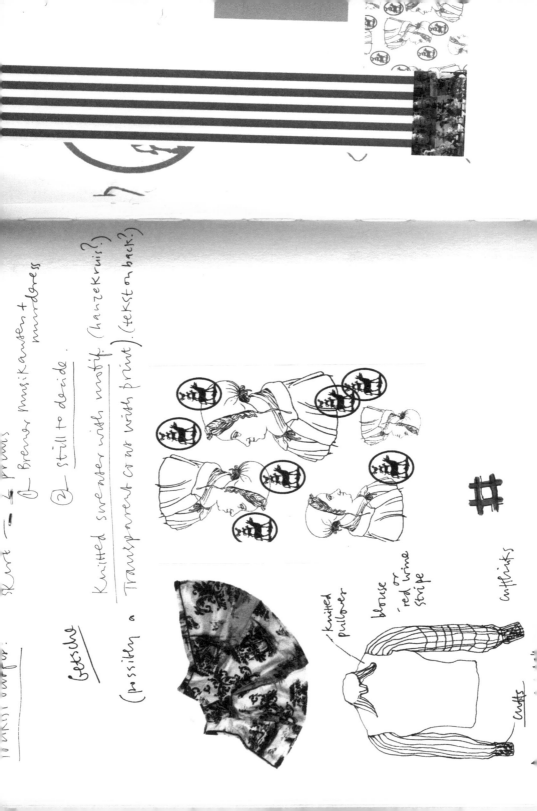

10 PARIS outfit:

Skirt = 4 prints
① Bremer Musikanten + murderess
② still to decide.

Getsche

Knitted sweater with motif (haarekruis?)
Transparent corso with print (tekst on back?)
(possibly a)

knitted pullover

blouse
red or wine stripe

cuffs

cufflinks

Outfit N

The style of these trousers corresponds to the traditional sailor's pants with flares and a high-waisted belt. Its blue and white striped pattern originates from the clothing prescribed for the prisoners in work camps during the Second World War in Germany. (In Bremen, for example, the camp occupants were forced to build submarine bunkers.) The loosely-cut sailor's outfit has an open V-neck with no button. The cut of the collar recalls a sailor's collar, but it is tied together at the front like a scarf. Its pattern is rather atypical for a seaman, as it is African in origin. (It is true that these materials are considered "typically African", but they are often produced in the Netherlands.) The text on the shirt breast is: "I should be at home" and represents a quotation from an earlier work by Tracy Mackenna and Edwin Janssen. The seams of the flared sleeves and the shirt band have a border with a line of text: "No man is an island". This combination is based on the idea of (compulsory) travel and expulsion, and at the same time it is a reference to the maritime tradition of the port.

The top is a brown, single-breasted jacket with open, frayed borders. On the back there is a large, green "14". The same number was worn by the legendary midfield player Frank Verlaat, who came from the Netherlands and played football for the club Werder Bremen until the year 2003. In addition, there is a wrap-around skirt (also sari), whose hem reaches below the knee: the borders of the length of cloth are crossed over each other at the front. Its brown and white checked pattern features the busts to be found in the Bremen Focke Museum. According to the labelling in the museum, these show the following individuals: Friedrich Wilhelm of Prussia (Crown Prince), Caesar (Roman Emperor),
Dr. Ernst Grohne (director of the museum),
Dr. Johann Albers (doctor and astronomer),
Dr. Dietrich Schäfer (professor of history),
Heinrich Müller (architect), Ludwig Franzius (electrical engineer), Günther Freiherr von Hühnefeldt (hero) and Dr. Johann Focke (founder of the museum).

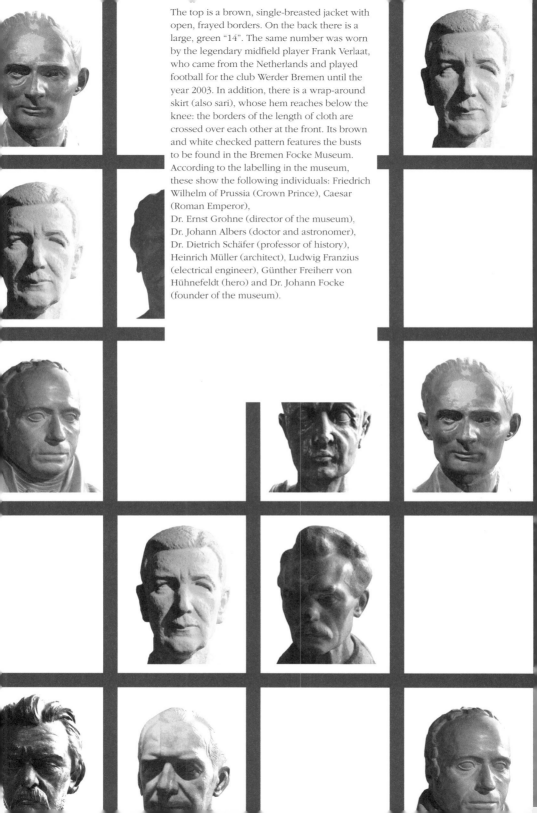

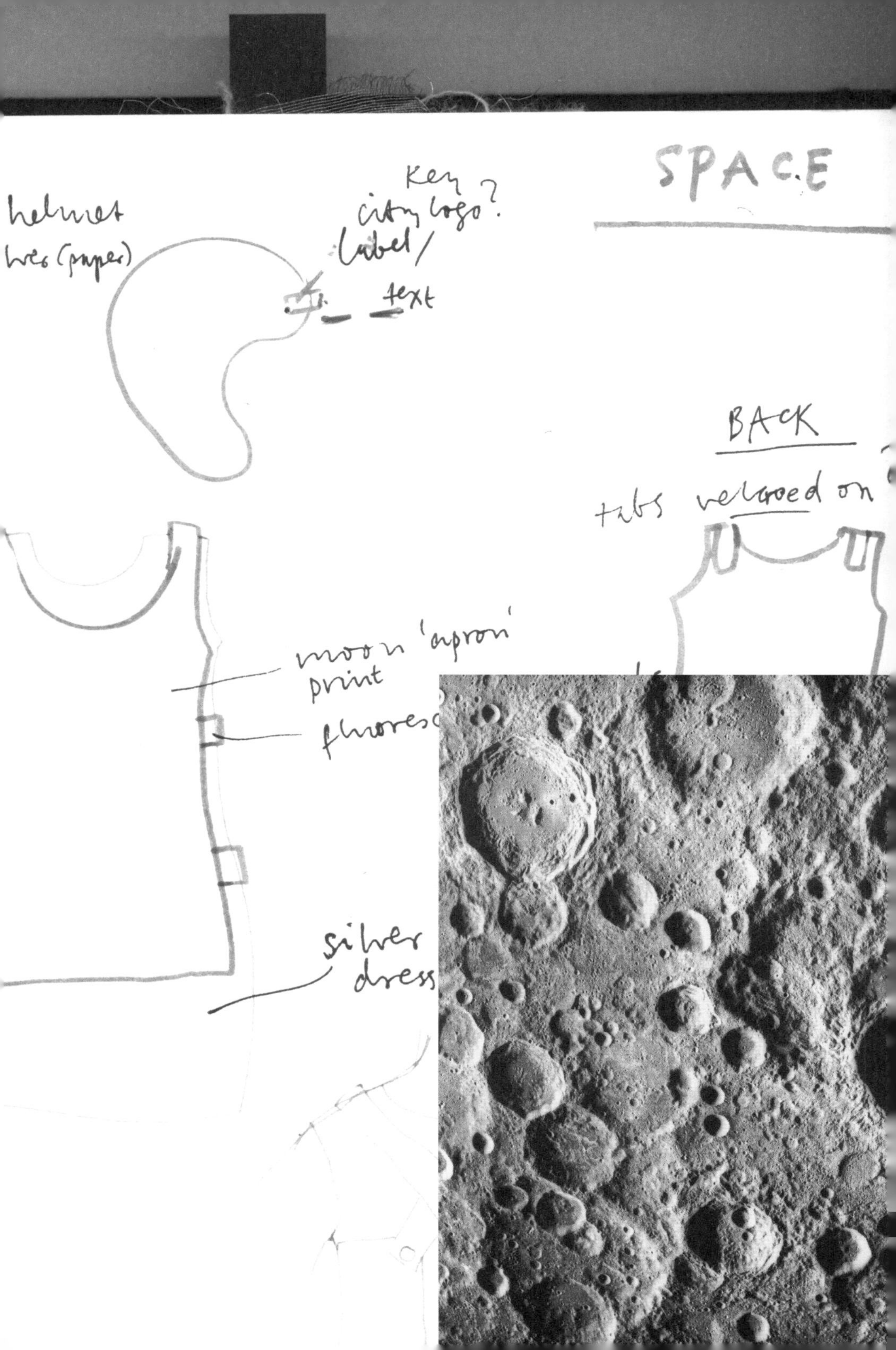
SPACE
helmet
lines (paper)
Key
city logo?
label/
text
BACK
tabs velcroed on
moon 'apron'
print
fluoresc
silver
dress

Outfit E2

This smock dress is made from two two-dimensional pattern pieces, bound together with yellow ribbons at the sides and on the shoulders. The front of the dress shows the surface of the moon and the reverse has a reflecting silver surface. A closely-fitting hood, fastened below the chin, and a scarf – 350 cm in length – complete the model. The scarf, made of baize with silver threads running through it, has a band of coloured letters worked into it, some of which are raised. They form three lines from a poem by Friedrich Schiller: RASTLOS VORWÄRTS MUßT DU STREBEN, NIE ERMÜDET STILLE STEHN, WILLST DU DIE VOLLENDUNG SEHN.

The poem is taken from an inscription over the entrance to a house in Sandstraße 5, which was acquired by the cultural society belonging to the Bremen cigar-maker "Vorwärts" in 1858. Its aim was to facilitate a comprehensive education for all social classes (especially for those who were excluded before). The model refers to Bremen as a centre of the aeronautics and space travel industry.

Horst Griese and Marga Baumeister

COLOPHON

PHOTOGRAPHY
ED AND ELLIS IN SCHIEDAM
Tineke de Lange, Tracy Mackenna and
Edwin Janssen
ED AND ELLIS IN TOKYO
Yoshihiro Hagiwara, Tracy Mackenna and
Edwin Janssen
I PUT MY NAME ON EVERYTHING
Simon Starling
ED AND ELLIS IN EVER EVER LAND
Alan McAteer, Tracy Mackenna and
Edwin Janssen
DIFFERENCES UNDER THE SKIN
Alan McAteer, Tracy Mackenna and
Edwin Janssen
WAR IS OVER!
Tracy Mackenna and Edwin Janssen
GROWTH, FORM AND THE INEVITABILITY
OF HERSELF
Tracy Mackenna and Edwin Janssen
THE BREMEN COLLECTION 2003
Frank Pusch, Horst Griese, Tracy Mackenna
and Edwin Janssen

AUTHORS
Rein Wolfs, Horst Griese and
Marga Baumeister, Tracy Mackenna
and Edwin Janssen
SECRETS ARE SAFE WITH US,
Tracy Mackenna, 2001

TRANSLATIONS
Gerard Forde and Lucinda Rennison

GRAPHIC DESIGN
Stout/Kramer, Rotterdam, the Netherlands

PRINTER
De Longte, Dordrecht, the Netherlands

ACKNOWLEDGEMENTS
The artists would like to thank Marga
Baumeister, Birgit Bekker, Lucy Byatt,
Horst Griese, Sari Hayashiguchi, Josephine
Mackenna, Ronald G Mackenna, Graham
McKenzie and Pernille Spence.

CCA would like to thank the Royal Dutch
Embassy, Entente Cordiale, Carnegie Trust
for the Universities of Scotland and Fine Art
Research, University of Dundee.
Special thanks to Tracy Mackenna and
Edwin Janssen for their enthusiasm and
commitment to the project.

PUBLISHED BY
CCA, Centre for Contemporary Arts, Glasgow
350 Sauchiehall Street Glasgow
G2 3JD Scotland

Tel 00 44 (0)141 352 4900
Fax 00 44 (0)141 332 3226
www.cca-glasgow.com

Director: Graham McKenzie

Published November 2005 in an edition
of 1000.

CCA is a company guaranteed with charitable status,
registered in Scotland No. 140944. Centre for
Contemporary Arts is supported by the Scottish Arts
Council and Glasgow City Council.

www.mackenna-and-janssen.net

ISBN 1-873331-29-0

CCA:

SCOTTISH EXECUTIVE

www.ententecordialescotland.org.uk